Colin Simms — Selected Bibliography

Lives of British Lizards, Goose and Sons, Norwich, 1970.
Some Effects of Yorkshire Flooding (with J. Radley), Sessions Book Trust, York, 1971).
Pomes and Other Fruit, Headland, Sheffield. 1972.
Adders and Other Worms, Headland, Sheffield, 1972.
Working Seams, North York Poetry, York, 1972.
Bear Skull, North York Poetry, York, 1972. (Revised edition, 1974).
Birches and Other Striplings, Headland, Sheffield. 1973.
Modesty (Swaledale Summer), Headland, Sheffield. 1973.
Pine Marten, Seven Prints, Genera 14, York, 1973.
Horcum and Other Gods, Headland, New Malden, 1975.
Jane in Spain, Genera, Newcastle-upon-Tyne, 1975.
Photosopsis for Basil Bunting, Headland, New Malden, 1975. (2nd ed., 1986).
Rushmore Inhabitation, Blue Cloud Quarterly, Marvin, SD, 1976.
No North Western Passage, Writers' Forum, London, 1976.
Flat Earth, Aloes Books, London, 1976.
Parflèche. Galloping Dog Press, Swansea. 1976.
Otters: Ten Seals, Genera 16, Newcastle-upon-Tyne, 1976.
Voices, The Many Press, London, 1977.
Humility, Spanner, London, 1977.
On Osgodby Cliff, Curlew Press, Harrogate. 1977.
Windscale: Four Cantos, Genera Editions, Newcastle-upon-Tyne, 1978.
Midwinter Housewife, twisted wrist, Hebden Bridge, 1978.
Pentland, Shadowcat, Weardale, 1978.
Some Company (Tea at 40), Genera Editions, Newcastle-upon-Tyne, 1979.
Hunting Bunting, Luksha, New York & San Francisco, 1979.
Ingenuity (Wensleydale Winter), Shadowcat, Weardale, 1979.
Spirits, Shadowcat, Weardale, 1980.
Movement, Pig Press, Durham, 1980.
Time over Tyne: Poems, The Many Press, London, 1980.
A Celebration of the Stones in a Watercourse, Galloping Dog, Newcastle, 1981.
Big Cats, Islamabad, 1988
A Second Book of I Look at Birds, Genera Editions, New York, 1981. (2nd ed. 1989).
Cuddie Cantos, Bellingham, 1986/7 (2nd edition 2000).
Eyes Own Ideas, Pig Press, Durham, 1987.
Luigi Pirandello: Navigator, Shadowcat, Weardale, 1988.
In Afghanistan: Poems 1986-1994, Writers' Forum, London, 1994. (2nd ed. 2001).
Poems to Basil Bunting, Writers' Forum, London, 1994. (2nd ed. 2001).
Shots at Otters, RWC, Reading, 1994.
Goshawk Lives, Form Books, London, 1995.
Bewcastle & Other Poems for Basil Bunting, Vertiz, USA, 1996.
Otters and Martens, Shearsman Books, 2004.
The American Poems, Shearsman Books, 2005.
Gyrfalcon Poems, Shearsman Books, 2007.

COLIN SIMMS

Poems from Afghanistan

Poems 1986–2009

Shearsman Books

This third, expanded edition published in the United Kingdom in 2013 by
Shearsman Books Ltd
50 Westons Hill Drive
Emersons Green
BRISTOL BS16 7DF

Shearsman Books Ltd Registered Office
30–31 St. James Place, Mangotsfield, Bristol BS16 9JB
(this address not for correspondence)

www.shearsman.com

ISBN 978-1-84861-255-6

Copyright © Colin Simms, 1995, 2001, 2013

The right of Colin Simms to be identified as the author of this work
has been asserted by him in accordance with the
Copyrights, Designs and Patents Act of 1988.
All rights reserved.

ACKNOWLEDGMENTS

A little more than half the contents of this book first appeared in
In Afghanistan
(London: Writers' Forum, 1995; 2nd expanded edition, 2001).

Some of the poems in this volume previously appeared, often in earlier versions,
in the following publications: *Angel Exhaust, David Jones Journal, Harry's Hand*,
in the collection *Big Cat Poems* (Islamabad) and in the anthology,
The New British Poetry 1968–1988 (London: Paladin, 1988).

Cover drawing of Ahmed Shah Massoud by Maria Makepeace.
Flyleaf: a page from the author's notebook.

Contents

A few lines of doggerel for fawning dogs	13
For I came to find the great Afghan Falcon	13
Nimble the men on the ridge, and the woman	13
Stoned steel rings a scream of distant rubble	15
Since shock for her children, collapsed, she is older	15
Millet	16
No Ants Yet, This Sand	17
Slowness, Baiting…	18
Vibrations	19
Hemipenes	20
He Paints Himself with Ochre	21
Remembering Embarrassment	22
Grafted onto Any Stock, Such a Bud	23
Refutations	24
Flustered Clumsy-Custards	25
Matériel at Herat	26
[Kalash]	27
remembered here, where Basil's Villon	28
The fifth-column ahead	29
For Derek: Terek Sandpiper Two	30
United Service Instruments Ltd., vs. Universal Scientific Instruments	31
Tumbleweed Originated Here	32
The Atrak to the Oxus	33
uncertainty, the notion of heavy-walking of old	34
sick of shooting Russians	35
rivers rise, torrents to rend	36
South east of the Black Desert, Kara Kum,	37
stones dry throat rumble near	38
Carrion	39
Afghan Bloodscent on a Dry Wind	40
Mirrors beyond Mirranshah	41
Thrust-mountains mightier but Alps	42
Claiming	43
Atrak Arcs, Oxus — mobile dune systems	44
all toward a sleep: a right sleep	45
Yardang	46
Creases swept clear by war	47

Higher than limber lizards—timber only	48
signal-tapped as a lute traps	49
The Caspian changes its shape every day, flickers	50
The being of being hit is it—	51
the only true necessity	52
Faces, Facing Disturbance	53
while The Distance implodes visibly	54
Ground to dry	55
All war in us	56
Fragments urging	57
Expectancy shocked at the first of their dead bodies	58
As the South Pass divides	59
I was with Ahmed when we found Abdulla in the desert	60
Hot Trod	61
Little (pre-Enclosure) garths	62
Kirghizia and around Afghanistan	63
The day has brought less wit	64
The only Christian in the village is…	65
Earthquakening	66
balletic twisted ballistic	67
All Hindu Kush, all High Places stammer	68
A Song of a Rocket-Carrier	69
The grounded swift feels feathers lift at the passing of wagons	70
Sandgrouse	71
Afghan Falcon	72
Three Places in Afghanistan	73
(this place is moving)	74
Rudaki, Tajik's Poet	75
Turbans	76
Altai Falcon	77
saplings elegant out of bare-rock showed	78
Some Khirgiz	79
Joseph Dalton Hooker 1848	80
Into view reminding of inner Utah	81
In a Sandstorm	82
(Uzbecki)	83
If you spin a very lightly lubricated ballrace, no pitted balls,	84
lizards downwind with us stand over stink off carcasses	85
as scent off sage flats	86

the captains look around the hangers-on	87
Airagain A Ger Wears Better Than Boozah	88
Cold—region's Snow—Pigeons plunge, forge-	89
(Central Asia)	90
(Hide sanded, Hider)	91
Snow Leopard II	92
For Abiz, Qa'en	93
Like we set the cant of our pikes	94
mountainsides in some places seemed a motion of grains	95
Liberty (Not Ever)	96
(in mem., S. Dillon Ripley, 2001)	97
There are no nightjar-nighthawks…	98
Nanda Devi Nanda Kot	99
Dry high tableland, tufts in its cracks…	100
raven echoed by chough in the cleft cliff	101
Not Disdaining Carrion	102
where blue bharal sheep trails band	103
who are you, that I see your face everywhere—	104
Nanga Parbat	105
the youth, I saw his ankles first	106
(Village hit by Hind rocket attack after Speznaz assault, Panshir)	107
Far skymarks and landmarks we claw for	108
Aftershock	109
'Zinc'-boys get	110
Fear	111
'Warbrede'	112
While rhythm we had we let spin butterflies	113
Within that shudder of other heat	114
Barcans II	115
Somewhere above, the ibex or some such is travelling,	116
Beyond a Desert Lark, sounding strangely loud	117
If not immeasurable, abstraction Grand Canyon, say	118
Apart Is the Moon There, Is / Obeisance	119
…There is a rind upon the arid mountains……	120
(As) Going to meet E.P. / about 14 years earlier	121

Dedicated to the memory of
Ahmed Shah Massoud
(1953–2001)

The author in Afghanistan, by E.M. Makepeace.

Introduction

In the course of my work as a naturalist, I've been able to visit Afghanistan twice in recent months and this tragically torn country, not for the first time in its history, is a scene of devastation amongst starkly beautiful mountains and deep valleys. Afghanistan links Middle East and Orient in many ways, Central Asia and the Arab lands, Russia and the Indian sub-continent, but we have little awareness of it despite reports from the war now seven years old, despite the visitors there from this country, the refugees from there now in this country, whose reports our "media" ignore. Large parts of the interior are almost empty of people; the better little farms of the bottomlands have lost stockmen and stock, arable reverts quickly without irrigation and care to windblown semi-arid wastes: generations of work lost.

Colin Simms
Low Woodhead,
Tynedale 1987

Distances open up, dizzy altitude. White peaks and silver edges dazzle all the while at which seems as distilled off glaciers as the rock dust on dry gorge, ridge wisp, kiosk and minaret alike all also appearing friable as cake in the mirage or haze dazing torrents and waving willows and tilting strata and stirring stars.

    I wanted to look, amongst other things, at rockthrushes and a mysterious "brown falcon". Some editors and "critics" dismissed my 1980s visits to Central Asia, including Afghanistan, as merely more exercises on the "hippie trail", an itinerary I had avoided in its time. Not so the *SubVoicive* readings in London or Bob Cobbing of Writers Forum, who reissued these poems and pieces in an enlarged and revised second edition to the 1995 selection. Sandie Robbie and Mary Hider word-processsed this version very generously.

1995

This work derives nearly from verses and sketches noted in draft or drawn during visits almost a quarter-century ago, and versions in the two earlier editions from Writers Forum. I have not been tempted to include many pieces started since, some at the stimulus of eyewitnesses now refugees in England I have met; drawn by a word, their gestures, a look about the eyes; accounts 'confirmed' in our media or theirs sometimes and often not; the few exceptions are obvious. I regret I have not been back.

Dedicated to those indicated in these pieces, and others who have encouraged and helped me over the years, especially now the late Eric Mottram and Bob Cobbing, editor of Writers Forum, and faithful former colleagues Mary Hider and Margaret Hartley. Nothing is included here not sparked off in Afghanistan, but a series of poems in the "big cats" (1988 publication, Islamabad) and another from Bamiyan have been excluded for other treatment. Even so, editing may not have been severe enough. The excluded poems, and faunal lists made in the Hindu Kush and Pamirs, are available, as yet unpublished, with subsequent essays on such topics as the bigger Afghan falcons, and the post-2001 Afghan "scene".

2013

A few lines of doggerel for fawning dogs

In a recent mumble-grumble our outgoing Laureate
—stuck-in-the-stationary-Establishment-Motion
complained he'd not been sent out to Afghanistan
—another frustrated Romantic Notion?
—another cossetted opportunity to spectate?
He could have done as I used to (even I could afford)
and taken the, educational, bus from Bradford…

2009

§

For I came to find the great Afghan Falcon;
what it was whether it fit as companion
representative of the great world falcons
for an arid and snow-desert mountain land
I found the familiar Saker mainly—and
the great-falcon features in its hill-tribesman
whatever his breeding, unspoilt he is a khan

There's dignity even in the vultures of these skies
they share with eagles, so there are always eyes
whether I saw or distinguished aright I was seen
by more falcon-formed people than I've ever been…

§

Nimble the men on the ridge, and the woman
with them; her bundle the lumpiest Khurgin.
Armoured-personnel-carriers stumble
aerials tremble some course-correction
snailpaced, tabular, radulas fumble
rumble half-tracks polished of friction
leaving whitened and silvered trail quite certain.

§

Stoned steel rings a scream of distant rubble
though slow to crump à la Krupp, shrapnel fountains.
"Over 200 Afghanis to the dollar!"
has become dust, fear's avalanches of
troubles with the rest. No interest in roubles
deserters loaded with them; but guns are better:
scorch over Kabul other than unburnt hydrocarbons.

§

Since shock for her children, collapsed, she is older
Rezvan has corkscrewed a supply plane down, certain
it was hers; though she had some help with the launcher
sore shoulder after, no ammunition to rehearse
decants the boozah tenderly, with thanks arising
is no bolder, neither bolder nor "wiser", will die to a tank
eyes ease the company, forgetting her curses.

(For seven years the Soviet 40th Army has only been able to safeguard the highway and the two pipelines north to the border and so on into Russia. They have not crushed Ahmed Shah Massoud's strongholds in the hills though they have rushed their crack troops, tanks, gunships, whole flyways of migrant planes to bomb and rocket from Kabul and from deep within their Union. Moscow's Frunze Academy has trained hundreds of guerrillas who are now bushed in foothills they haven't learned every inch of and their tour of duty is over before they do—if they are going to).

1986/87

Millet

Sign nearby: there a boot has been
terraced cereal mine-field
where (prayers flag wind)
rags rip, torn plastic roars and rattles.
scarlet, emerald shards attract…

Pharsee carefully phrased salaams
undulate the outskirts with the prayers
parsing dust to some ephemeral dune

same wind can trap careless minds
unless the eye learns, spurn the false
feet guess a few steps to a new tune

quartering for particular lie
sorting-out stipples, wind ripples
stem slack or taut lines, lying-in of mines
shadow of mine sleeps with my own heart
no beggar's tap, no blind man's trust
a child was taken away in ragged parts
no children play now, the plough grows rust

used to seek lizards and larksnest, stare
where weathered quartzites have been disturbed
the cast is reeled in over a signed surface
ground grasshopper basking as secure as ever
dither spider, uptilt barrels spinnerets gossamer
same wind tell-tales to its anchor the wire
chimes thin as far muezzin off minaret, and higher.

(Between 5 and 25 million anti-personnel mines and wire triggered, grenade booby traps have been sown and planted, especially around villages in one province, and by both sides).

No Ants Yet, This Sand

Earth otherwise unstirred tip-crisp inch-perfect
here one graved raze by noise-wave either shell or rocket
displaced a little way, laid humped, glazed as clay disparate
some isolated deep-plough turnovers cadavers displayed
seamed transversely as if ancient, grain arbitrarily running
dismay the thrill and turn of the blood and of guts.

So cold for burnt cloth, the scarab already burning, laces
to the faeces, but the wind shifts a little into our faces
taints the lump to the throat, bundles, and blood pulse races.

Slowness, Baiting…

slowness, baiting the "Bird of Prey"
ground baiting day after day
proves he's a vulture really
not to be compared with
Altai's enigmatic falcon.
whose contribution his play
speed, as a windy day,
good for "saying the say
recurring wordslay
carrying life away
at the right moment"

Vibrations

Antique air-conditioning still working
fans for no Afghans!! and no punkah-wallahs.
Antics upstairs: "drug dealers and gun-runners"
sounding like martens in farmhouse attics;
revealed as those scene-stealers anywhere
Bradford-related Pakistani children drugged or
lassitude paranoia adrenaline hysteria.
One of them: "Mahsood has got back
the emerald mines. We'll trade them for guns".

Peshawar, from Dean's Hotel

Hemipenes

Mountains pulled these winds scraped pushed men
beyond these foothills and no further such
forks grain up into the Hindu Kush
deserters from Alexander's battalions.
Rock's serpent's Organ-of-Jacobsen
between delicate placement and sheer "luck"
tried them for genetic fit, and they stuck.

He Paints Himself with Ochre
(once man, now bird)

Does he do this as Tibetans do, against the cold
and or against insect attentions?

Majestic Death is the Bonecrusher
most magnanimous of all vultures
power for his transmutations buccaneer
changes light and shade post-mortem
gives his life back to mountains

Yet mean to us in his appearances
his watchers say avoiding Russians, Russia
offers fresh unexpected reward to such
as we are, Ins'allah, not "familiar"—
type of man isolations control over
with the eagles ours against life grievances
for similar wisdom, long life deliverers

Leaves patter for half an hour after
death as if dropped by the Bonecrusher
spiralling, or falling faster charred
the flash of the dump going up
going up had not sent him away
or its earthshaking crump or cordite
bitterness full on his air hotter
than ever, buoying him up an hour thermal gyre
longer than he would have hung there watching
so that we watched him for when it would clear:
go in and crush skulls ahead of him.

(Lammergeier: The Bearded Vulture)

Remembering Embarrassment

reject impressions on the trails' silent
possessing the way which is less direct
and because of its weight not to be detected

fearing is still not open enough, this night
we move in not even in bright moonlight
confession will not wait interrogation expected

Hindu Kush and beyond, Pamir knot and beyond
divide stars, near and far, dislodge the way
their procession this is, eagles' could be wisdom

part of it was cast off from the mountains
part by the head of the man ahead, for the moment
or age our leader, whether tomorrow he *will* be different

one stretch of alp will suddenly connect, recollection
happiest one man who passed it on; I hope to keep up
beyond where I have nothing to bring out embarrassment

then I find that like mine in the light their eyes
are on falcon, enlightened, and raven, anxious
caress and pat each burden and forget spies and foes

and sing in the evening if we've been able to go in the light
or in the morning if the day ahead is forbidden
denned grumbling bears cracking lice and listening!

and to EMZ

Grafted onto Any Stock, Such a Bud

Sage birds out after rain in pursuit of it
rive juniper bushes hardly if already berried
stone echoes lose old clothes to increment talus
cement dries around toes silences and pales if
chanting children as to stick-and-stones play
deliberate tune stiff as water-dropping, as slow
in starting-up early crickets above colour's sure notes
pure chords looted like a Ming bowl being used
by one to mix barley ground as shale flour mash
stark up-sun white-stemmed *Betula utilis* birch-
stick sings rattling thick black-lenticular marked bark
what is going to be written will depend, as with our birchwine
of Hesleyside and there less sweet, more stark;
on the *sap* running, if he is still here to sup it
who has long since discarded hashish and tobacco
and might be Kelly's young brother, back in America,
strapping expendable paper cups to cambium cuts;
premature "buds"… all such children never grow up.

Refutations

Bare ridges bridge
rubber boots rub-amber
screeruns creeks as bergs age away
loosening smoking rooftops pantile pattern
Shiva lives high Himarleah, other
gods regime the rivers
are other mountain-clusters refused to climbers.

Flustered Clumsy-Custards

Our way decided of a thousand trails
mustered arbitrarily (according to day and season
and safety), moutonéed rock old as of Cumbrian
rockribs similarly worn down by feet and sheep
rock at the surface leathery, (not meadow-hide dales
collecting rain, mist, seed-clogging bootseams and eyelets)
but noisier counterpoint, stinging bare hooves ringing steep
inselberg's; Schoenberg after 1914 when structures
emerged fresh as for Pound, all art broke strictures
"brave are those who accomplish deeds beyond their courage;
if the Gods had granted their awareness of what they were doing
they would not be so enviable, but what they do is to be coveted".

Matériel at Herat

Walled locality, more corral
than city, more man who can
rebuild a gun of any material
come to hand as the only ground
we have is the day we have

spiritual rationale and its optimism is
temper to appropriate calibre

crankpins grimace harness lynchpins
as turned earth home yielded silky as spittle
bronze palstave supposed millennia "old"
uncreased, smooth as of constant use
shepherd claimed he had lost it "only in the war"
metal never old until its gone to corrosion.
In this war, makes ore of filigree, decor.

[Kalash]

Islam came only after Sikander
Alexander was before Islam
and some of his men wanted to stay on
and grow vines, to everyone's wonder.
Kalash of the Hindu Kush their children
before the Hindu were killed on this mountain!
Buddha-Gautama before the Hazara
came with Ghenghis, Uzbeks, some others.
Tajiks killed English as they now kill Russians
Uzbeks also; even Hazara and Pashtuns
—and you tell *us* the tribes are scattered?
No-one will beat off the Northern Alliance!

§

remembered here, where Basil's *Villon*
runs in the Khurgin Dillon-
Ripley's *Thrushes*: his and Ali's
—more than comforters, these privacies.
Basil gone, Dillon to report to
(Reg Wagstaffe gone, Meinertzhagen
rubbed out by Derek Lees-Smith)

such men show in men's faces
long after they are bones in their places
Eurasia and America, in common

illuminated prisms Wrens
Rock Thurshes, wintering Blue Robins
spare my blushes the bear in bushes
must know he rocks between

§

The fifth-column ahead
as for the Nazi take-overs:
her husband, home from the war
to a shattered harvest
found his wife had tended the cattle
done all she could for the land
They broke her bones and raped her
do the Russians know how he became a monster
and did they know the heaviness of his hand?

For Derek: Terek Sandpiper Two

River creepers rasping
reluctant toward Caspian:
this week off Wanney Crags
I watch Wansbeck elect for the North Sea.

—young man sprang on
from the platform
at Peterborough
as bringing one in
onto the Carrier
Britain still is
this week he is over Libya
a few hours, but he remembers
Wanney Crags as the Badlands;
he is off a farm in Nebraska

"ask me no questions of F1-11s"

River seeps into its sand
and undermines terracing run of blood off dry rock
corpse rucks, relaxing
mountains have sung after it
until losing sight of it,
murmurs into the embraces
careless clutch of matter-of-fact;
crescendos soften the distance
sand on wind to a croon of Koran
"lullee, lullaaiiea ease me
nothing today, just see
why I am here. I am
Terek Sandpiper of Enehan"

United Service Instruments Ltd., vs. Universal Scientific Instruments

The ancient British optical instrument
I used, they prized above the German
or the Japanese and as robust as the Russian
but, we agreed, only sharp at infinity
like the best hill-man's eyes, the eagle's.
Better in the dusk-haze than "technology"—
a one-hand weapon, or bound to a gun.

He'd been in the re-opened mosques north
in Samarkand; "the best ornament
is always out of sight, except to God
and the eagle", then kept it twenty feet ahead
of his feet, on irregularities in the sand
wind brushed, or by some speznaz' hand bush
the instrument, experience, God had kept him whole

the other hand at his groin, and not so steady
feet in each other's treads little column.
One jabbered of the rattlesnake's threaten
—trained for the (universal) work in Oregon.
It's no more than the goalkeeper keeping goal
not knowing where the strike will come, but its near
nettle-grasping simple with boldness, on your mettle.

Tumbleweed Originated Here

Sex may be sacred in India
In Afghanistan it is interior

"the heat of the skin comes in
prevents it from coming out again:
poetry, war and love, superior".

From a shambles of rambling desires
one man smothers, fires up the others
one man to lead is enough because
only one man will know himself,
clear sight for the long-distance fight
the one man without any brothers.

Barbed wire razored Russian
influence only steely snags
as of the steppelands northward
abundance, but blowing from nothing
more wiry bundles across our senses
tap, rattle as flags, sherds
trap, yet as wind does words.

The Atrak to the Oxus

sun quarters Kara Kum
running checking all null
noting nothing left to chance
but own hardly owing plans
stuns stone hammered stove-enamelled

butterfly-opened onion-skinning pulses
continual anvil-tapping invisible tinker
exfoliated himself on his own persistence
impermanent pulsing presence an existence
mirage, convincing clinker skin expansions
metalled-road hoax, over sufficient expanse.

§

uncertainty, the notion of heavy-walking of old
winter sun dipping behind hills shaking in the cold
silver rays loth to stay

you feel the spring running-over, back at home
Gandhi's precept: not merely negative harmlessness
but it is a positive state of doing good even to the evil-doer
it means the putting of one's whole soul against his will—
Patanjal: near him in whom non-violence has taken root
all beings renounce enmity.

what it is to be thirst, and quenched
all the civilisation came because
men cover their heads; "even cowboys"
we will have to learn to live in the desert we came from
therefore what the Russians have done to his village, his irrigations
his stone house, does not matter

§

sick of shooting Russians
he was, already;
tapped at the wounded
armoured personnel carrier
shut up like a can.
one side; he had
as the smoke cleared, suddenly
dropped his grenades over the other

the spin bowlers' wrist action
googly or chinaman
opened up the can
bat beaten by the ball before

all the armour faces forward, he'd said
"shoot the chukar from behind":
from under the overlappings, red.

§

rivers rise, torrents to rend
incorporate breccia
abandoned caterpillar-tracks
(silkworms, remember)
talus-cone volcanic with mines

"Russians want to capture you reporters"
"You's be more use to us as
camp followers; and we don't need them"

The shelling dies down and the echoes;
mountain-thunder sets-in instead
no damage but dust, the markahz
had been taken out long ago:
this was only an exercise for us

(but Mujahed Kedir has lost his mulberry trees)

§

South east of the Black Desert, Kara Kum,
is Kizikum, "Red Desert"; Central Asian
sand desert grows by rotting in patches
waterhole-marking scrub and bushes;
tufts seem to fit a pattern at speed, arising
torsion, the arc turns only at walking-speed
short shadows along outcrops copy terraces

for M.H.

§

stones dry throat rumble near
stones avalanche unlubricated, tumble
crescendos of Stravinsky's Rite of Spring
driving surprises, but inevitable
after that silence as when lightning had
cleared the glen, the TT Norton gone over the Mountain
a silence feel ears steer
for sound, wobbling the jaws
the whole being readjusting in fear.

for R.H. Clark

Carrion

Steppe-Eagle in winterquarters' turquoise blues
bas-relief on turbulence shuffled into distance
sick of hoping for pouched-marmot out of his burrow
drifts, but on a progress buttressed by bluffs
the sun also catches, caches hibernacula
one snake too late, latched-onto, due,
waiting to die under the weight of sky.

sand-cat after "ground rats", serious fun
not in sufficient haste to waste them
on a fine wiring line over open terrain
quarters it visually only less than the harrier
by scent more so, before it evaporates
like our will to go on by the same sun
yawns at the same some invisible barrier

finds our thrown "off" meat the bird had missed,
we found the place he had squatted and pissed
a quiver in the sand like side-winder's shiver
shuddered in our mood, lifting laughter!

for Tom Callaghan

Afghan Bloodscent on a Dry Wind

desert light limps from the mountains
their winds droop and decline, a neckline
a skyline descant on a penny flute.
(wet dog's-mercury in wet spring home woods)
proves as immaterial
cotoneaster, hackberry, rosehips define
neither gorge nor craig clifting Yarrow
dry loaded Kalashnikov, he is wetting
getting warm with his own decomposition
too far down the ravine to have been retrieved
save by the raven, even the "brownneck crow"
for the lammergeier surely too narrow

for Tom Pickard

Mirrors beyond Mirranshah

Not Alpine Swifts
all day harsh swallows Waziristan's
creases cracked clay ring uneroded peaks
and ruck pure defiles unscanned

boundless ranges engage
sawtooth straight-cut gears cut out in silence
who saw fifty years before it came here, the mirage
restive ratel ratching, on bear rage

autonomy is by winters-impassable
men by narrow paths over and roundabout
taxonomy never direct—waves of warriors—
the privilege is, even war is partial, but "all out after the Russians"

Karakorum seven hundred miles impervious through Hindu Kush
in exclutch eggbox hachuring
extended life sentence and oviparous pension
Pamirs loosen best gearboxes, tighten and tire suspension
coil the births of creations the snake is viviparous
a mechanic as Lawrence was is a man of virtue, but porous.
Heartbeat as of Indian Enfield—everyone's scansion
increases with gradient over burden;
his shot under honeybear, allowing for distortion,
Ahmed said "Could have gone anywhere", outcome uncertain.

§

Thrust-mountains mightier but Alps
with India wedging, instead of Africa,
underneath them, then up
even K2 may still be gaining height and is not the summit
already climbed, nor is any other;
yet it is eternal as mother of the snows
bed making nurse-mother pushing over the folds up the heart
making comfortable tea-cosy of a continent,
breaking beds open as clouds of its own making
sliding fractured-limbs of folds onward as nappies, nappes
gods see all or are unseeing, playing about summits.

Their distances localise storms, alter light, colour, darknesses and winds
halfway-slope, shelving outcrops,
cliffs, crests, deeps without the sockets of lakes or craters.
Unseeing themselves, as the mountains need a spirit in them,
each a different spirit as the mists they generate themselves
are varying and come and go but are except in the clearest season
especially of the night and of the dawn

For Mike Shayer, climber.

Claiming

Village headman, claiming a hundred years
had seen the British beaten, wants to see the Russian beaten

    stranded on a broken headland bluff,
    remembers me Ruskin, painters' stuff and poets'
    waiting for the moment, Islam is before Mohamet
    God will move their patrols on, ignorant
    we can bounce even our ideas off them

    I am happy to watch for the wheeling birds
    while there is light to see the shades come on
    and the mountains change colour smoke stains

Yet he is more aware of all round, than I am
the other, the great blue-brown cliff where the birds sit
all hills are intimate, every mountain is a hill
manageable to such men, and having such men in it.

Atrak Arcs, Oxus — mobile dune systems

Bahcahn, its urging windslope in motion saltation
stinging salt crystals squeaking quartz, silica topple
each grain surging, singing, ellipsing, arcing ripple
not finished ever, the snaking crest tumbles over nipple
rumbles and stumbles little golden crescents ever urgent
Kara Qum silver lappings in the moonlight, khakis sun stipple
reflects bits of its own winds to topple in reverse
top edge trimmed sidewindings, its crest at tangent.
Wind curving carving testing never arresting argent
as wind does not let the arrête rest; Islam at a canter
each piece is handled, even the tiny dreikanter
I find in lazybed-garden under the postglacial rind
that wind sand-blasted blank, cold-desert marker
facetted similar little pyramids pre-set familiar, movement.
Split-mathematical crumbs will relent to molecules
compelled precise apparent random sillinesses
dither downslope, accumulate to be barged into stillness
alone and echelon on recall of drumlin, ledgers lava-pillow
contracts signed, handed over, accommodated, fulfilled for
moonglow without wind, their word sings a moment.
Withered is landedge, for this is sea, sounding tidal
tons of mass-movement over-riding, men slide into mankind
schools of these dunes' energy store, swells spell scroll
the hope of motion high-lines lope of a frozen ocean
there is the Expected One still in motion where no-one follows,
nomad the only hermit-raider not over-ridden, hidden with what he stole
stalks hermetic the wolf alone, his fellows in the hollows
howl for the outrider, hide sanded, all spoor blown.

to L.C., Bellingham 1987

§

all toward a sleep: a right sleep
even wagons caravan

mountains indifferent, canvas
paralysed, parallel suns' lie
this high-plain stains by

sunshine after 'summer' stumbles
extends a deception. I am from where
touching the summits is all that is needed

Islam is by trade, from Gangara
The clouds are blue; Arapaho and Hazara would
recognize each other!

for M.H. (October 1986)

Yardang

channelled   arid
day-stages   caravan-overhang
dune-circles   transitional rumpled   cricket-flannels
we are chased by sawtooth windsharp escarpments
herald sandpiper piping us along intervals, processional
but through sandpaper storms   confined in its and our rimming
lyre saltbush set by limit-gauge gouged tenon-saw gorge
baize and baige
tunnelled age

whether winds which corralled   lithographic accord
tradewind no slate to be wiped   but heaven records all
code of variant notes chorale
frustrate with its own load   tried to decode
for the sandpiper   echoed   her sharper call
concentrated its extended parallels more metaphor
and actual decision within ruling clifflines
its own rare floods would erode
debris of centuries, teeth set on edge

Scallop and overchute, cornices
in ecstasy with fallen keeping station behind
for what we might put up
tunnel canyon familiar oasis   parchment palimpsest leather
desert's own guardian arid or garden
welcome amongst the frettings, sheer palisades fused together
immaterial grit absolute in her generation
the browngrey blue falcon to sit
else had only season the eyes for it

Magdalen Wood, Undercliff, 1987.

§

Creases swept clear by war
strain silt from irrigation
faces leased to grief
retain lines for common-sense
"look, this is what I meant:
Russians, dressed as civilians,
are killing us Afghans!"

coppered skies sheen over mountain gleam
clarity of brilliance needing no stars because of faces "can all America
have more *people*?"

But such people; the Californian girl is partly bare
and no one will expect other of her because she does not care or know
        anything
I am allowed my hair white, and my beard
and must know *something*!

for Maria Makepeace and Eric Mottram

§

Higher than limber lizards—timber only
where sun southerly-aspect lower slopes warms
linger skinks the colour of silver lichens
links polished to schist pebbles' richnesses
with hints of inkings and the pink flankings of slow-worms
suddenly tongue-gun at lethargic larvae—
lasiocampids', grasshoppers, lowly forms
Güldenstedts, and Black Redstarts go for
all so intent on the hunt they ignore me

§

signal-tapped as a lute traps
galliard of wind in tablature
but gives sittern
metal strings orpharion few leaves ago
a song of the way passed for purpose
not only not to forget the journey

the pace recognisable in all hill-men
there's no other way than the will's
contouring time to gather thoughts with them

hit by hailstone or spent bullet
either, out of a clear high sky
until you see, miles on, the clouds that lie
massed behind the wind and that high stile
beyond the ridge whose furrows have filled the whole day
as a great lizard stretched
but one in the short stride of a woman; "her" load
temporary shame to lame to blame Russians
(rarely even heard of a herder's woman)
"look", they said "tidy!"

for Heather

§

The Caspian changes its shape every day, flickers
like Bonneville did, or Lake Pickering
the belly dancers here are tucking-in to their knickers
the only wildcat probe for tricks that with explosions
the industrial spies picking fluff from their microphones.

1942 Hitler thought it would win the war for him
but all he got was a whiff because of Russia
America is pushing the Caspian into Turkey
which is probably not good for Azerbaijan
the oilfields are far from exhausted though
Baku's tycoons included Rothschilds and Nobels.

§

The being of being hit is it—
to be or not to be is not in it
fear after is, a mesh of reason
no reason for it;
bit, the flesh
is a soft net
shells smell, but the bullet…

a burst in the air is singeing hair
skin whistles singing it
after it a moment
at last the fear
takes the spit
because we like it
polishes, nourishes a bit.

trading-in spent Stinger-tubes
with reluctance; such useful material
in a better time had made utensils (parts also for a time like this!).
After having been shown how
the wobble within
when you are not sure
you know what you are doing
not sure of its effects anyway:
coming down the Lord's Rake off Scafell
meeting a different woman
not quite telling the truth.

for A. Laskar

§

the only true necessity
our hearts know
perversity in compulsion
is to love each other so

to the enemy, hospitality
home, art, so!
perversely; warmest welcome
invader, go!

Distant shot dispatches easily;
it *seems* slow.

N.E. Afghanistan, 1987

Faces, Facing Disturbance

Cleaveline down midline, sloping front and noseline
not into the strong chin, escarpments open to frostheave
grey eyes ride in great caves seal in caves of the sea
waving hair-curtain thin but eloquent
stranded on a brown headland bluff proud
of sand and air
resulting surviving guardhairs
bird-like turns of the head
man used to air and distance
turning accentuated by head-dress not turban
nose a hook to the angle of the nostrils
falcon's cere
each stiff moustache fine
with little twizzles of twine
blue-brown cliff where birds sit and come in,
blue-brown dome and tower as fine.

(for Ahmed; his face)

§

while The Distance implodes visibly
"no difference from Czarists"
and its expatriates leave off patronising
and are often more "ethnic" than the locals
who are already less islamic than expected
the old animisms have been celebrating as ever
being not, to be resurrected

a few stone circles
but the country needs a blues or two
to ring true toward purples
perfecting process of turbulence
let the wrinkles comfort the faces
slow, and dance
percipience

(for B.B., obviously)

§

Ground to dry
to hold or to die
thirsty

does anything die on a desert:
mountain, no cover
whose life is little
jewels under stones

except in dust-blows
to let bones grow into

ground too dry?

§

All war in us
at the desperation
if not before

monasticism of going to war
going to work with Allah
heightens country-colours
and especially the night
drugs rivers to sing new songs
old songs within
their waters redden
rigs roar under vulture-soar

For A, Tajik

Fragments urging

…your glow remains in the thorn-embers
had been only kindling for the coals
this North country too much for old men
not like Siberia, even Altai-Shan!
After the death of the memory, even that
defiant for a while, a stife remains
wave-form, so it waxes and it wanes.

Slopes sun, stone-stripes on hillside
run, falcon-streaks shuffle on mantling,
according to re-ordering's requirements
and all lines focus at head and summit
these eyes that chime stones around them
Tiger's Head; a sign for India—
Hindu Nationalism, headless river

sheer liquid power in the West!
Confucius has of the study of odes
they sharpen the eye to see Order;
bird or tiger, improve mind to remember
names of all, for power and philosopher!
how the only worthwhile advertisement is concealment;
the bold, hidden while he stands out bold, elegant
in himself is thus himself and only then himself
so that what comes unbidden is this wealth—
a soul; one wanting to save, demanding it.

§

Expectancy shocked at the first of their dead bodies
its rocking-chair swelling blown, big-footed
stiff leathery, skin as dromedary,
owned by the earth already, her scavengers'.
The first wounded bodies stutter another momentary glaze
some of their eyes give me comfort; gaze
unexpectedly quieter than (Wounded Knee):
crueller than the assassination
(less pitiful than the dishonoured girl dead by the highway).
mutilated, or the one on the dunes who'd put up a fight
no one claimed to know whose daughter—they tell you what you are
quicker than the fox, eyes glazing under the hand on Blencathra;
than the otter shot in the water, they tell you, inadequate reporter,
to draw the tanks out into the open; make sure of each one.

§

As the South Pass divides
and unites East and West Rockies
Hunjara divides East and West Pamirs
Karakoram Highway only it states
thread of many Silk roads, millennia
West India by rocky defiles to China
a hundred and thirty miles from Gilgit the boundary
the post for checking travellers and for barter
the only trade over the pass but exchanging cultures
so take it over, Gilgit, silk maybe for Kashgar;
tea, surprisingly, goes the other way, westward
trucks as permanently decorated as Vardos
leviathans for avalanche and landslide
washout and snowmelt flood, roadside
the unclenching of the great fist, knot or lingam
Tienshan, Kunlun, Hindu Kush, Karakoram
squeeze each to Pamir lost at their apex
the Old World's Roof shedding mothers of hills
caravanning yak flocks beyond the metal
move as sorely baggy panted as herdsmen
the New World's rocky heart more barren
will as naturally take on its Buddhism.

§

I was with Ahmed when we found Abdulla in the desert
who had gone aside under a green tree (he said, just to pee)
or we'd not have found him so freshly dead that no squirt
of scent at forty degrees had given him away, and his bravery
his brothers with us soon had his price in a Russian shirt.
They told me they knew because he had not said to them
(hurt, they knew not) it was to pray, the hour he left them.

Hot Trod

light violet velvet
hirundines' and bats' wings
dark bar vulture aloft
tobacco and other sweet smoothnesses
move along a hard hillside soft
conspire to empty it of other figures
moonlight might have similar effect

and a whole armour has passed
particulate, wrapped (but Rievers)
no single man can be assassin
no gleam from any barrel
by her satin hand one is a woman
no Steel Bonnets, little harness
loads shift at a foot's jarring

§

Little (pre-Enclosure) garths
drystone cops boundary ridges
the height you would throw stones out of your path
Little tilled patches tilesheds
quarryspoils overlapping scales
feathering at lower edges roosting partridges
seen through colliery-row windows childhoods ago.

§

Kirghizia and around Afghanistan
"Boozah" is well fermented beverage made from "kumuz".
The Khirghiz used to be usually temperate
but there has been a slackening of late.

You take two pots, one larger than the other
and fill it with the kirmiz almost to the limit
and keep the lesser pot empty and cold beside it.
Light a good fire under the big pot, and fit
a tube from it to carry its fumes into the cold pot
where a milky distillate, or is it a condensate
is derived from it. This is the said BOOZAH,
oh I forgot to state
both pots are sealed with skin and mud—
It tastes a bit like POMBEY but it is different
and, the beauty of it,
if the next day you drink water on top of it
and nothing but water, so temperate,
you are tiddly again; it is immediate!

§

The day has brought less wit
and wisdom than a night will
that bird of prey is still little-known and rare.
Her hands
caress the ledge-bird onto its distant perch
peaks stop staring
and corpses out there
starry dark stiffens stuff
breathless, doubled up…
staircase and pubic hair
all wandering exploring is
for her, for the women not watching.
Swatches of a rare mustelid
better than a medal at the R.G.S.

The only Christian in the village is
one of the survivors of sudden carnage.

(the village still burns. The centre will hold
in the grip of an open-eyed widow, stilling
her heart through necessary slipping, into the bold
—a censer-swing from here)
but from over there where she (wrecked)
grieves her loss, throwing back neck
then head, again opens eyes against tears
answer—catches his soar and turn on its beat
thermal nursed because war wrought more heat.
Caught more beauty than brought desolation
—scorching cross across this one Christian
he's flinging ring within ripple-ring, screwing
not spiralling, hope driven home, renewing one alone:
prehistoric maze-rings hewn in hill and stone,
hill fort, back home and the note in this silence
averted from her suffering, deferring observation,
this bird of prey may be asleep on the wing.

(Northern Afghanistan, 1986)

Earthquakening

                          the shiver after
shock   even if you are hot
you have to recognise it at once

                          surviving danger
                          then elation, ever joking
                          an affinity with fightingmen

an ultimate feeling which cannot be spoken
                              emotions even for the non-aggressor
                              situation seizes what it can;
                              you must make it take it
                              you are a lucky man, and if you are
                              make it work for you

§

    balletic twisted ballistic
    'thunderbolt' fossils in Bellmanbanks
    rockets impact, perhaps as much to persist
    as belemnites; a matter of scale, the rock indifferent
    part to be absorbed into matrix, shot first yet not insistent.

    Forward observation-post
    reports slowly back toward Khost;
    there are men on the mountains in-between with radios
    in touch, if intact, antennae alert their high cwm
    show no exercises that they are under fire
    the long crimson flash comes, thin as wire
    the dust and darkness silence, for all the boom

    crump the soldiers are no further from
    trumpeting our presence, anyone
    with a good telescopic sight, or our eyes
    could have picked off at that distance
    and few will fight beyond their own valley
    those that have one. I tally with surprise
    only three of four now, from their stance.

Bellmanbanks: Iron District, Cleveland.

§

All Hindu Kush, all High Places stammer
excoriating hill-bulges, slough talus-cones
cooler and more attentive than I'd imagine
imaging then for the sketch book before they shift
turf-bending, only apparently-glazed surface
glasspaper and patterns of goat terrace, frost
pulsed as sun expanded to geometric effects
same as the Navaho noticed. There a hammer
like the Marxist emblem, here a, Crescent, sickle,
conventionalised Kalashnikov dithers into recognition.
And we all, the weaver said, have faces like 'crows'
"raven", or (stronger) "vulture"* …listen to the stones trickle
but under what foot? Stuttering of the God
whose face is thus revealed in skin of outcrops

[*literally, "eagle", but the scavenger was implied]

A Song of a Rocket-Carrier

'Write this in Correshushka'   the field   OK, Shushkacorree
write this hill path   thin file brings to mind
railway line, tracks-taken-up   dust disturbed but redistributed
Incline up to Blawith   climbing shines under shift.

Fahad he swoops of feathered tassels   flies by Steppe Eagle
sleeping swing   yielding   cross-contouring quartering
shivers a solid-quiver shower of lead   to be but blunted
no Front but cells   pockets of resistance enough aslew, shifting.

Ahmad grabs jagged as Jugger   thornpricks open and close around him
arm swings once for all that   aorta trails   a lamp puffed out
retreats on a vein   of one shout   stiffening, the frontier is within
spaces   where there are no places   hamlet is a blanket thorn over it.

Long grass waves   rocket ejaculates   blind comet singes
noise only then coming-back   shivers before echo's track rocks, sings
black apparent on contact   neon, then steel   breath exhaling
mountain line, unchanged chain   must be as deft goad to Russians
                                                                      up the road.

Blawith-in-Cleveland has an old mineral railway.

The grounded swift feels feathers lift
at the passing of wagons

angle continues   curve in span   carpal's deflection   but impotent
fan of finger-thrusting spin   wins only its own wind
gapes silent screams   only circumlocution   looses no choice of
air
let along sky-writing   all effort is less than its meant
trajectory
projects less than a few hieroglyphs in this dust   but, at least, *curves*
grounded more eloquent than I've seen thus on concrete and asphalt.
Lifted onto turves, hardly a wall; throb into flight light as flames' dance.

(nr. Isfahan)

Sandgrouse

dovesoft, grouse coarse
linking pigeons with gamebirds
Syrrhaptes, or *Pterocles, paradoxus*

Kirghiz is
forty miles between oases
and grass-seeds

these birds squeeze
sphagnumsponge undercarriage
for young to *suck*

Afghan Falcon

on the dust thrown up   by her passage close by
by dry broken bowl-shawl also of, rim of, this Basin
two vortices undulate as the power-strokes clip up and down
as horizontal as her flinging-flying   unlike the pigeon
whose downstroke makes an elliptic whirl series as a whorl—
the swifts are likewise though they scissor the air more
    yet leave a similar path   a pattern in the air

tracing in the motes of his morning's canyon
the sun's rays   inclining only steadily from near horizontal
like a swimming auk or cormorant makes under water
using the wings torque more fully than often in the air
the rush of air on the ground upstroke   buffets the Lahore fans'—whirl
which had been less efficient, of more drag, even the car evolves to reduce
                                         turbulence behind.
long range sniping this bird takes the rodent without adjustment,
                                   every stroke a stoop.

Three Places in Afghanistan

I. (In Herat)

old rose after heat	man who can build a gun
heart in a corral	rebuilds one
not a pretty walled city	out of anything to hand
yet	which is as spiritual
crankpins grimace	because we look down
without groaning	at harness lynchpins
axles are greased	for him to temper

II (Anonymous)

Birds come up first,   the shock   and even the smoke
a scalp up off the village that
a halo in mirage   but just dust and smoke
the blood and wine run under   (all)   the Russians cannot plunder

a year later near the same place   a man's head ringed
with scar-tissue where his scalp had been loosened, has worn
his crown of blood "a week without washing it off" blackened
ageing slowed down; the raid could have been last month; not last year
but he still hasn't found Her ... and he still grows no hair

III

the camera does not allow the photographer see unless he is *The One, Rare*;
"let not your words by polished for the page"

(this place is moving)

(this place is moving)

a bus but more of a truck
decorative as a temple or a tomb
wherein you can tell which are mountain men
more by their bearing, less by their smell
carrying well the sprung rhythm of their room,
their space on the trek, their silence as stem.
Lurid the contrast—Pakistani film stars stiffen
pasted on wings and tailboard   Wanted Men
sides and doors consistent of other graphics
"better to be mistaken for a Nuristani"
Many of them look like Imran Khan,
"lucky to be with so many of us"
bicycles carrying 2 or three, and Honda fifties;
but MZs can be made to carry, easily, three—
"they make them well in East Germany"
alloy dusts away instead of rust
overloaded with a community goats don't trust.

Rudaki, Tajik's Poet

Polyfilla'd pillars lean   in tension   fear
Look close—Rudaki's rick is loose,
Caucasian marble in the Firdosi Library, Dushanbe,
pediment threatens an avalanche   near
            Shaky mountains rear
shelve rubble   under thunder and we
feel accumulation   topples civilisation.

Whatever it is, the tricolour is not for "tomato,
mozzarella and basil"!   Rezvan says
"sunrise, high snows, irrigation".   this old man
"desert, cotton, and the garden"   or the red
is the bleeding Kizikum opened   forever leaching
its oil bleaching its strength. Poetry's silent commotion
the green—the mirage fertility yet springs the oasis.

Earthquake eloquence echo chiming process levelling
even the young man will not shake divinity's sting
seem, then loom up and nearer when the air there is clearer
not going-away in blueness, eternal high-snows alter
mind toward infinity—put bluntly we don't travel alone
for we are not travelling; it is the distance in motion
flickering gullies run sudden their slickensides…

(1987)

Turbans

Then spears thrown, one at the other side almost out of sight
the other replies; and no one is hit but with the sudden thuds
arms were as to ache from shield-hurt and some old days are
new darts here, and nothing of either is new if we list dread dead
as were there then: apply the same epithets as old enamels craze
and the singer also is honoured if his new angle gives truth
without seeming: finding light in the ways of warriors' minds-set
dignity scheming—   in expressed honourable patterns found.
Helmets disturb: but bare heads are not seemly even for snipers.
Dust clouds arise; dither in eloquence, as mists arise at home
giving away the lie, careless and consequent of such broken ground.

Altai Falcon

Banner and banner-bearer of Attila singular
one poised over the jugular of all the Old World.
Hunters in hundreds for hunger of the Great Khans
successively, but back to their distance, best of bounty
hover impressively, indifferent, wind-dance irregular cavalry.

§

saplings elegant out of bare-rock showed
crevices and holds, every slight shaking
earthquake's eloquence foreshadowed
foreshortening geography, serpent's quaking
levelling and looming, in microcosm
familiar, every sheeptrack its own road
widening in shale slickensides and bosom

already passes seeming narrow as a man
gorges rope-bridges or fallen tree can span
as insecurely as heel tapping loose rocks
crags that can tap-tackle confidence to mantra
here as in Sicily rears that finer sense
which deals a wisdom out of ignorance
which in the mother-earth's providence
best for its mountain moufflon, *Capra*
one step at a time, and testing chocks
gravity or split hoofs fit in crevices
precisely amongst "dharma" evidences…

Some Khirgiz

many had been isolate
on a roof of the known world
relatively left alone mountain state
their Pamirs until the '78
invasion by Soviet military hurled
gunships, shells out of their air
over fourteen-thousand feet to tear
a pastoral peace well to the northeast
of the Afghan elements and fusions
some had already fled collectivisation
and more now left toward Pakistan

I came upon a remnant, like other ones
on trails of tears and like the Cheyennes
and Arapahoes unable to adapt
or unwilling and increasingly trapped
in the south, some such place as Oklahoma
tried to emigrate, some succeeded, to Alaska...
some to the mother-tongue cousins in Turkey...
moral movements to try to keep an integrity
leaving a few on their long-loved pastures
with some fraction of their former cultures
not as demoralised as on new Reservations
for the land their land is what they breathe
and need to be themselves. I heard an elder seethe
before he laughed, and told me of the vultures
going away for want of carrion, "but the eagles stay"
who love our sky as we do, though it is emptier
as the land is and the eagles say our culture
will come again out of the earth the marmots' way!

§

Joseph Dalton Hooker 1848:

"Vapours raised from an ocean
whose nearest route is more than
four hundred miles distant
are safely transported without the loss of one drop of water
to support the rank luxuriance
of this far distant region.
This and other offices fulfilled,
the waste waters are returned by the rivers to the ocean
and again exhaled, exported, recollected and returned"

There as at the end of the monsoon,
you can believe this is the foothills
no ghoral or serow, ibex or markhor;
would Hooker have noticed the stone spreads
and that within the cobbles semi-desert
the concretions demanding splitting of a sample
to reveal the same genera or families
of ammonites as in the Yorkshire Jurassic
spring-flush of flowers, summer butterflies dried off

§

Into view reminding of inner Utah
the playas they here call 'tahir'
basins dry and smooth surfaced in summer
shallow water or wet-layered in winter
desolated, the desert never so deserted yet
what one of our number terms 'numinous'.
Then they told it was here they put to the sword
every living thing in a village, during tribal wars,
when there was a village where just a few stones
courses, an irrigation channel, mark the shore
but an ancestor of one of us survived "by prayer"—
no-one then would kill anyone at prayer.

"You are not here to verify, instruct yourself or inform curiosity…
You are here to kneel where prayer has been valid…
The communication of the dead is tongued with fire beyond the
        language of the living.
Here, the intersection of the timeless moment is England and nowhere."
    (from T.S. Eliot, 'Little Gidding')

In memoriam Jean, d. 1980, immediately after visiting
Little Gidding for the first time (40 yrs.)

In a Sandstorm

broken images suddenly blind
as variably dusty air sullenly deepens
a chasm with little warning mined;
much of this land looks like limonite
scattered shrapnel of natural shatter
glad of the plateau after defiles
tight quartzite and silica speznaz

enveloped each of our narrow places
under sun to a pinpoint, and gone
shelter downwind of the smelter
pillar-advanced of dense cornucopia
"current-bedded" graded grit and sand
silt and pebbles the permanent stand
whirling dervishes of past millennia

pushed-up from the south, the columns
of mountain-building, rim-armouring
shredded our threadbare, reddened
windburn, wrinkles astir after storm
and on again comes the calm warm
out of the void beyond, croak of raven
and I find some of the fallout is pollen.

speznaz: Russian "special services"

(Uzbecki)

Donkeys for hire have bitten back the junipers
(shepherds back home blame for illness in sheep and cattle)
Gurdara village of graves along the Silk Road's roughness
few tourists bother. I went round this village, its dogs
like avoiding William Beck Farm at home: Disturbance
more trouble than it is worth if it is transmitted nuisance

Timurian Samarkand: its sand-dunes mined for gold
told of the Russians; noisy and busy as forge Sheffield
cottonbelt Bukhara the crossbow of all the world
but building-sites and then their facades. As of our backyards
they want to go back, those displaced, even to Siberia; hurled
across space as if it were time. Only time parades backward

when the trouble will come here, few will fight beyond
their stumble, shilly-shally, bounds of their own valley or
the Fergana. But the 'best' of them, which are the worst or
reckoned worst will have the will and because *they* can
Toyota Landcruiser, not Landrover, driven by a man with his foot
off from plastic strives over the mountain heaps only its thirst is

An owl will watch by night, nightsights. A vulture will
watch by day, saying nothing. Certainly not prayers, for long
(neither knowing a safe house). In between is no wonder
but is the extremes. All else is (everyone's) camouflage. An age
hides in another. So suddenly, yet repeats some of its passages
so there is time or room for one wise man, to be killed yonder.

§

If you spin a very lightly lubricated ballrace, no pitted balls,
in the echo-chamber of half-a-crankcase fast for several seconds
you hear the song, the body of the song after its lyrical start
—that brief start-up against the inertia of the race (and when it stalls
the falling-away in a splutter at the end of the song, the *becknan*
of the cock Black Redstart and also Güldenstedt's Central Asian Redstart.
So I smell the oil again whenever I hear the unlikely call!

§

lizards downwind with us stand over stink off carcasses
increase attend vultures version of iceblink ricecharger
in wreaths smoke chokes reeks sweet (sweating horses)
—heavy flies in close-up rose up; weak vortex
or sleet slant: seeing death (unwillingly) it is chilling
aspic temporary, Ants loosen pants lice. Gorse
Basil said, rattles like ice in the flask, donkey dry flanks

as scent off sage flats

    I've no illusions that much of what follows will not be poetry:
    I learn my trade by fits and starts in seas of anxiety
    and too much straining after meaning betrays my other sort of training
    and even most rhyming cannot be sung even in the graining
    imposed going over trails, mostly rough terrain and high
    to catch breath to further butcher even intake and sigh
    transform the hill walkers' rhythms of colloquial speech
Some of my upland becks and burns in the far North Country now present
increasingly the debris of erosion in their currents' content
and signs of the arid. Sand and rock flour coming down with the peat in spate
fewer fauna evident, and that goes for the land they drain. And I rate
reductions in wader populations up there, other birds', lower intensities
of insectivorous mammals, of beetles, of butterflies, of dragonflies
of frogs and toads and newts, of lizards, to the same causes, and have data
over the decades to support such observations. Return to it later…

§

the captains look around the hangers-on, the warriors and other personnel
an apparent Indonesian; two inspired by Peter Matthiessen
a girl fossil from flower power's generation, quite without reason
stuck between California and Nepal "stretching a saint's toleration";
with a few free-lance 'journalists' determined to see some action.
Beaten out as of hot metal on a foothill shaped like an anvil
the morning takes shape, a coulter to divide us, a prow for the ocean
of ranges and peaks beyond. Which of us for decision determination
not in our hands, only appearing arbitrary. "the caravan" for Renville,
Santee Sioux, thirteen years earlier "will not take more"—for cohesion

1986

Airagain A Ger Wears Better Than Boozah

under the zone of the blackgame
still at twenty-miles-an-hour breeze
where I'd hoped to find the falcon
disturbed the sandgrouse just the same…

yeast-grey, as arid westward ancient
and alai—is there really a ger-falcon
calling and I can't see it yet even yaks
the mountains fringing the Gobi are *old*…

creased, wrinkled, sage, not as bold
thyme scents, link arms in front
this village no less than Namarshin
it is a different kind of cold.

that of grasshoppers and quail
greasy-grass, crossed, back east
but only a juvenile Saker

felted welted straggle the 'shans
in there? somewhere an eagle stands
seem cowed and so appear familiar

as Khazak faces, facing each other
'Cumberlan' style wrestling thrives in
but my identification is this—

Nenthead
For M. Shayer

§

Cold—region's Snow—Pigeons plunge, forge-
temper their passions, into the blueing gorge,
So deep and sudden at speed the hawk,
which knows them their thoughts/missed;
we marvel time's interchanges with space,
yet watch him later close, coldly engorge
on a finch over torrents frothing kisses
over seething immersion of this emptiness
stained of iron slabsides of urinals' grace.
As came up from nowhere it's ethereal dove
to translucence against the real snows above.

(Central Asia)

slide down the stairs of the sky
successive racks of rock ledge and scree
steps of the earth. From miles high
in sable and carmine a ceremony
in black and red, repeated sighings
the tumble of choughs bumble past me
echoing each others' grumbling and cryings

mind I don't come off my edge
into the gorge all is narrowing,
winding the message back up the wedge
I know only the earth is hollowing;
deepening their emphases soften
merge octaves lower, intervals slowing
meaning I overlook often

is the ritual; flickers of flame
leading choruses of feathers
trailing and steered by the same
red of leg curves. All tether
mountain to air, earth to height
redness to blackness, bird to its name
sounding right, rounding out in sight.

1986, rev. '07

(Hide sanded, Hider)

Wind itself does not shift such lichens
as rosette-stones rich translation lonely. It
rises gutsy low slung gun-runner, scales lifted
once reluctance rubbed off eyes after my persistence
and had I gone on a foot blind it hadn't happened

for ounce occasion such as this must merit instep
effort enough, and measure, whose lope is pounce
and open-country's fetch and carry, harrier's quarter
controlled flow, to stop instant, back into the stones
coating them still, but with just that coati lift
of the long-tail tilt which has my mind drift
off again, recalling cougar and cheetah…

Snow Leopard II

…your flow remains in thorn embers
only kindling for the coals …
North-country now too much for its old men
not like Siberians, and under Tien-Shan.
After death. of memory, and its threat
defiant for a while, a stife remains
wave-form, so it waxes and wanes.

Line cloud-striped sun, stone-stripes set in hillside
seen from above, run shaft-streaks settled by mantling,
according to taxonomies and taxidermy
all lines to focus in face and summit
lichen like those eyes which chime stones around them.

Confucius has of the study of odes
they sharpen the eye to see such order;
names of all for power until extinct,
how the only worthwhile advertisement is concealment,
the bold is hidden whilst he stands, elegant:
is himself in himself and only then
neither leopard nor tiger, nor ocelot nor lynx…

For Abiz, Qa'en

shattered, Khorosan's scattered archipelago
once island villages are now their archaeology
foundations swell show only when the dust settles
downcast-wave /sand erases carpets on cotton and faces redden

fresh mass-graves warm humans before that first-sunset
sudden-yellowed   even aridity
saffron acres / fields yield   and wheat-on-the-stem
and the fallow over-stressed

Aftershocks-baffled   pillars, storm swept His Will
will stiff ruffle   riffles and ben and silted slope
battered back to rocks in the sum   fellowship hope
gone beyond dust
blessed familiarity beyond dust   and strong as poverty

when and where eleven years ago uttered
                unsterling hospitality
                "Come Again to Qa-yen"

as comprehensively rubble as if the Russians had hit

Earthquake devastated Khorosan—places and people on the Iran/Afghan border I visited in 1986/7 and a family I stayed with have apparently been wiped out.

(1998?)

§

Like we set the cant of our pikes
by the nick in the hill guiding the westerlies;
us, our hay; others, their barley-stooks
so I'm up at night for the smoke-flap's poles
"wind that will find all the statching-holes"
as with any homely garment;
yurt or lodge is only circumstance.
'Hoop of the people' spins
skies and stars round all the circle
thin skin never quite keeps out of mind,
awareness; a thought rises, trout, to find
time ready for rippling the circumference
we are passing through, few of many mansions,
migrants to no known destinations but this once
and one: the round earth our home and not our home
yurt and lodge both speak impermanence.

Scarth Nick (North of England), 1950s
South Dakota 1970s
Central Asia 1987

pikes: haycocks

§

> You came out of the night and took our road
> and made it gayer than the dancing wave,
> you who were bright and beautiful and brave
> —Bill Cowley, *Tara Devi*, 1942

mountainsides in some places seemed a motion of grains
seamed dry spring-sapping of
                            benches, elevated plains
what other was it you could hear but their diurnal rolling
expansions and contractions, destruction's gravity's gain
burqua, kitay: and chaplis—yet this woman is only bone and skin
but also life in the eyes: all I can see of her grim—grin
these families of three and more toil lightly to the passes easier than I
more lightly than some proper mujahedin, melons blessed with heroin.
Women and children's burdens greater weights of good and of suffering

(Some birches even, juniper, poplars, maples and planes
many birds, some other animals the same)

as if I'd already lived there, they said
I had a good eye for khosht and sanger
"Yes", the leader said, "like other cliffs
these rocks are only *looking* perpendicular"
"Tik toktu…" then the drift…

stiff limbs loosen and at first lighten
and the night itself lurches into motion
the little movement of distant avalanche
that touches only our noticing, not imagination
weariness swings the load to the road, looking askance,
camels look and feel like this, groan at the goad
mind sets, relinquishes watches to outriders…

The shock they felt reached our faces
then it reached our feet
and there was then the strokes of artillery
and sight of the smoke of it.

Liberty (Not Ever)

Fled on weakness, fearing speaking and questions,
bad fettle, on an impulse southward;
Parapamisus or Parapamirs riz' red
Arthur's Seat's, Saddleback's, Blencathra's, Haystack's Bed
familiar fetters suggested, seeking anonymity
"nowhere better to find leopard, they said
in all Afghanistan", or, Turkestan / as nearby
[for that matter, Uzbekistan too and near enough to Iran]
"you can go back as freely there as from here: a man
might be as few as a leopard [to follow one]
how Robert (the) Bruce reportedly put before honour even
and much before glory the uneven Liberty
but which of us, then know or knew what he meant…

Murghab River rises in Afghanistan
(Band / Turkestan mountains), a river
collecting rivers northward only to
lose itself in the Kara Kum depression
except that it leaves some salt(s) on the air
to leaven the sand, and may even reappear
some season at intervals rare and queer

Band / Turkestan Massif, 1986

for Derek and Dillon
Afghanistan 1986

(in mem., S. Dillon Ripley, 2001)

my passerine work on your hunches
loth, but ravaged by my falcon
your thrushes. Fall in the mountains
opportunities to study must come
and must come in rushes …
corpse-scavenging charnel
with us, museum; he had instructed us

lizards downwind spin on it
with us stand off
stink of carcasses thinly spread
increase attendant, ravens, no falcons. Link
vultures slow wink version of iceblink
of ricecharger wreaths smoke chokes
reeks, sweet…

heavy flies are roses in close-up
weak vortex, sleet slant elsewhere somewhere past
seeing death chilling;
alive, ants loosen pants lice. Blown, as gorse seedpods
rattle, ice in flasks, relieved Bunting's desert donkey
panniers at sunrise, mine help the climb

Malakand Pass

§

There are no nightjar-nighthawks, and there seem no 'flies' for them
where over these arid badlands arrows gleam, die too soon
to be studied arcing through, though the spyglass is ready.
They say stay, for the millions more there will be next moon
knowing none of us may be here—the eye and breath steady
I notice most of these ephemera rise in the east
showers or singly, though their directions seem random

Where fireflies never seemed nearer than across the creek
comprehension misled stalls at even narrow spaces
late short morning strode the ranges appointing peak to peak
soon high-level swifts are sun's vortex of arrows' graces
until full, each bevel falls in sequence into its hollow;
the earth receives what she sent forth to replace the stars with
while, idly attentive, we prepare the goat for the feast

Tchai and the night, new perspectives explore for lice
monuments have to be seen, and who can declare for these
eyeless or blind, another goat apparently blundering
because the suns socket is burnt black to its lees
amongst stones, desert baked stones, broken-surface voice
safe for the slither, once only, of a serpent's santering,
garnish. Read while you can. Forget not the casual least.

Nanda Devi Nanda Kot

mightier thrust up than alps
restless India wedging
north instead of Africa
careless rucking under-edge
buckling advance every minute
so that no height can be the summit

mother makes clouds form like no other
snow-mother making beds we sully
comfortless tea-cosy of a continent
grinds fractured limbs of folds up and over
each other. All seeing or are unseeing
gullies seam out of the mists they engender
as only one of their winds is warm, insane
—the same that brings they say monsoon rain

We held up at the halfway slope, shelving screes
outcrops we dazed at remembering the Ottercops
and rhythmic sequences in gritstones and shales
there unseen, but here the lone marmot sees…

for Bill Cowley; Tara Devi

§

Dry high tableland, tufts in its cracks, but I'm stopped by a patch four cricket pitches width and length; littered bleached charnel and something in this recognition itches broken bones, whole bones, no bird bones, mammals from yaks' down to marmots' had seemed stones scattered by some storms or by a giant predator's strength.

Or did these all die in some mighty depravity; most of them robbed of their marrow; air, sky-burial in the sense there of gravity; but spread randomly. One white stain urea, and with the dark centre indicating ejection from a great bird's healthy venter.

Though he hasn't come today, and he doesn't come tomorrow, all of my Russia can wait and watch the sky of sun, stars, sun from the break of day bowlspread to the gathering of frost whiter than his discarded empties, for he is the bone-crusher giant bearded vulture-falcon-Lammergeier. Here he comes for bread…

(Scriabin's 'Poem of Ecstasy'; this ossuary)

§

raven echoed by chough in the cleft cliff
closing in darkness less deep than their's
(which show a starker force of nature
than geomorphology does, short of a crater):
look into this cliffs crevasse where there stirs
upward peremptory guffaws on tainted airs
cold only redolent of what must run below
the torrent unseen and unheard but fellow
of us more than of them; to evaporate later
whereas the crows go nowhere and are not less
for being fewer some particular part of the stress,

Not Disdaining Carrion

Bluffs show; dawn's own dust roughens stuff,
light strengthens hoary night's still story—
sand-eat's after ground rats sullied slough.

Teeth ever here and the arab-hookbeak scarab-stones
for fresh dung and carrion. Shadows rear over talus-cones

Horizons basins fight raw light into colour-bands,
right perspectives rumour Himarleah as nomad.

Carrion remains. An *Aquila* of faded epaulettes is
heliaca rather than *clanga* and never *chrysaëtos*.

Bas-relief to feint-retreat is in our mirrored-mirage
distant clouds seem to repeat, turbulence blurs image

Steppe-Eagle in winter quarters!

Hieratic as Gaudier's plain facets, grandeur gawdier
Imperial Eagle high as haughty, nor *pomarina* either

Rush on, off, militarised mountains, off Hindu Kush
by occasional artillery puffs—Ahmed Shah's "little push".

For Tom Callaghan, 1986

§

where blue bharal sheep trails band
high contouring seams and stain
vein alum or lead, iron
thinly cling to steep, hardly scarred
daren't look down, edge ledge and scan
the line ahead   and   again
wary the less, way sure the wiry.

sinewed ribs stretch heights we never
even tickle, trickle sinuous rills
dry in almost every weather

night, stare into the flames
as blaze gives into the sun
to get the night-sight night long
"blindness" as the insight
from sundance day's daze

hot springs bubbling life
through evaporites
smoking surfaces
of dying furnaces
Moking Hurth stife

Moking Hurth: a bone-cave I excavated in Teesdale, North Pennines.

§

I

who are you, that I see your face everywhere—
but it is not ever your face, Afghanistan, or Eire,
something someone something I have known all these years
who can you be, until I have begun to know myself?

In the mountains, then you can see more clear
for the puff of smoke, hardly the din of explosion
as if a quarry far distant in Pennines or Appenines
so that the man here knows only its one of theirs
over where his brother died then, before the fear
not having heard its whistle which stopped our singing—
"you don't hear many men whistle now around here"

II

There is no silence; all is music if we can hear
some, a few, of the vibrations. We will respond to
a tuning fork distant across a room from one in motion.
A toy, the bit of the gun, for the boy with no toys
the joy he felt of it transmitted across the same room
a dull boom distant, secondarily delayed the realisation
that in its place it would also have to help kill Russians.

Nanga Parbat

for Bill Cowley's spirit and shade; who would have had me on this mountain twenty-five years before I ever did come, despite his recollections and his poems, at hill farmers' crack back home in Cleveland.

but the main delay is in the history
of the continent long before man came here
for this awkward prop-forward's shoulders
obstruct the course of the proto Indus
an Obtrush Ruck, but in the real long run
cannot prevent this mightiest of Asian rivers
collecting twice the volume, eventually, of the Nile
or taking the Gilgit, here its bulk—equivalent
tributary along with hardly any dissent
though their headwaters are a thousand mile
apart and each has the impetus of melt
and time and all of thirteen thousand feet
of solid, difficult, resistant Karakoram;
Indus, and Brahmaputra, rise on Kailas in Tibet
as Tees and Tyne rise together on Little Dun!
Indus has given its name to India
as the Tees to our beloved little Teesdale:
track to the lakes mountains of our youth
huddled not in the back of a van but cuddled
with rope and rucsac on the old Velocette
over Yad Moss and Hartside every Eastertime
and some-winter weekends in wind and rain/rime

§

the youth, I saw his ankles first
uptilt as tiptoe together, perched
shining a little in the clearing air.
All dust-covered, and dust descending
strangely though earth, orange earth

this Afghan, naked, 'all a man is worth'
buttocks a little parched or poached
shitestink value, and more than faeces
peaches or apricots rotting, though flesh,
grey he had seemed the previous night

Mohammad; they turned him over dead
with a quicker look at my eyes-ahead.
The muffled noise had done no more work,
absorbed in belly and ribcage and groin
all debt; yet his worth will be reimbursed.

Mahmood moved his tally-pebbles
fingertips sticky with blood, stumbled
words familiar already of Quran;
(umpire at the end, perhaps, of an over)
but we could proceed with no more trouble
that day than fumbles, disagreement
silence best measure, quorum not mine.

(Village hit by Hind rocket attack after Speznaz assault, Panshir)

        Once-was
        hot tile dust is as rock flour.
        Before it cools   coils
        boiling-mud oxidation in a like
        aluminium, cloth, vaporised
        oxidised more slowly, after
        consumption   no oils.

        Wood at
        touch is ash, sticks did
        split, spit boiling sap
        splintered animals
        marrowfat
        splattered pointillist
        blood is artist.

Blossoms smoke make
night shoots exotica
of rockets, of his mother
appallingly poked, soaked
in fuel; their erotica
pall spread lightning strikes
kiss is once. Sword of God
he said: Sword of God
his hand gripped, a hiss
rocking him. Throwing-up
later; to start left bits
of her, and of someone else
legless. Survivor(s) leg less
eggwhite straddles hill
and sill marked for Passover
burning sear speared across land

A furlong away, lizard and snail
eat each other, as before. Which is which
their molecular fossil (a while) again.

§

Far   skymarks and landmarks we claw   for
score and store: a section of stars, lost
is slowly regained, very slowly; its cost
stumbled sore feet in the darkness. At last
the col; smoothed by some ice flow once or
again and so shining back on some trust
beckons and beacons, corridor from the crest
but we are afraid of its open-ness and we must
track by its rocks and the cliffs, as before.
More friendly finally than other, than vast,
we have forgotten the Russians
     reason and issue for.
     But the mountains ring
the mountain wings offer looking or laughing
and at the back of this file a rocket-carrier is singing.

Aftershock

so that I touched the wild tiger,
why, but to "count coup" without harm,
eye to eye, his not seeing nothing
until glazed, almost dictated, over
as the purr arises up from the tickling
a young river's roar out of its torrent
at night, sudden lip of the gorge
warm and warming encroachment throat
willing away the chilling moment
years, yet napp on an unworn carpet
jewels, taken away from a poor man
half-closing amber round goblets
two-cloud drunk drool double sunsets

…what has brought on this canyon?
I open my eyes, my own eyes open
in the throb that relaxes all, and widen
eyelids and cornea smarting between eyes
as if at a fire, at my tears his eyes
his ears come forward in a dance-figure
individual, detached from their ground
his own quarry-face scents sun has found.

a Central Asian tiger

§

'Zinc'-boys get
sheet metal caskets
spent shell-cases
dead chrysalises

one in five of their
hundred-thousand
or seventy-thousand
come back wrapped

those that are/were found
some so mutilated
their parts unrelated
to each other. A round

number. Armour-piercing
stare out of softness
stars cut out of flesh
eyes gouged out fresh

cordite about but
throats are, all, cut.

Fear

fearing even the night
                                      we move in
Pathan trails putteed feet select   slape
in the wet   rockfalls to its slippery grave
        keeping erect with a burden
reflect obvious for secret
each placeman carries within (him)
                    direct to the heart of each woman
despite weight not to lose way
      not to be detected
             effective disguise at a distance
stretchridge toothed alp that will connect
with another and beyond, another offset
and at target yet others.
You must believe
      we get up from the rocks like coneys after the gunship has gone
for the bright moonlight to study your photograph in it
        tiredness
so we are never open enough   even in ourselves   set my eyes trance

      her eyes, at home, that had proved too cold:–

    the coney's   rocks pikas eyes had, crouched, fear in them

    as the gunfire shadowed crawled over toward the burrow entrance

'Warbrede'

(a 15th century work in the Pocklington MSS, No. 10)

Warbrede breeds maggots-blow
              rots dagg-tailed corpses

baggy breeches
              congealing the saddest flesh of all
              on the living faces, not under them, not under the skin

war-bred maggots glut the best of any, show
                    festive fastest warp
direct through pelt and weft
              sweetmeat dissolves bacteria
              into ground blood blacks to stir air sickening sound

beeswax clotting,
bulk the heaviest around
              rotting fruits not long litter
              hills, hollowed for sandgrouse
              slow humbles even we knock down

eat of meat now is not meet
              roast as it rots and teeth
hawk and fox boxed to the ground
              dead in each other's jaws, maws
              shot spat out broken boned stun less, browned

§

While rhythm we had we let spin butterflies
light new colour contrasts to fresh depths, of glows
obsession took, taken from, say, Berlioz;
shadows shaping, sharpening by, shifting by
repeats, variations, all surprises those
—developments beyond anything I've known,
disbelieving softer tones—dust laden skies.

Across the arid, weave between flower-stands
come-to-hand as easy as Northumberland's
vivid faces avid of need breezes defy
fritillaries as silly here as they are rare at home
and the birds in hot pursuit; the lizard and dragonfly
rustling in the same key on the same sun's salty shale dome,
—a fraction of this riot-life our limestone-pavement lands!

October 1987

§

Within that shudder of other heat
indifferent to time's other baits
mandarin on no street, she-bus waits
in her paints pants, jolly prostitute;
garishness can never be complete.

Gearbox mesh, most worn component
engages, perhaps full complement
no counting people aboard, livestock
and to no souls' correspondence.
Young girls, un-noticed mothers, dried fruit
Only obvious man stoned, replete.

Barcans II

Barkhanoid dunes tail-off into spots,
often ocellate, on a still wave-pattern,
an indeed-simple transverse-dunes' arc
ever the same Mecca-directions flatter.

There is progression in, of, shield-shaped barcans
scan a distant procession wander the erg
—rubbing by amber-snake, electron.

§

Somewhere above, the ibex or some such is travelling,
clatter down a few stones—can start an avalanche—
as sure as anything is the whole mountains' unravelling;
rattling Geology's assurance that every limb and branch
of these Hindu Kush is slowly rising up, under Allah…
reassurance of "their" nature? One whose caution spared,
he said, some less-than-surefooted buck for his long gun
because he'd smelt the heavyness of the billys of the herd
—and why, anyway, would we want to spoil their rut and fun
(the billys', that is) amongst the she-beasts, easily scared…

§

Beyond a Desert Lark, sounding strangely loud
this theatre lightens far, quietist sigh,
keeps heaped-up as towers of immature cloud
sky, sleeping over top-gallants, unlikely, high.
Curtains lift the middle-distance, ever slow
tilt perspective with, approach rear sky
widening horizons' perpetual snow.

Foothills enlarge their measure at a canter
folds drape to our feet, merge slowly serge to sage
and lift the censer, back-and-forth quarterer
cultivator of 'mice' below its Ice Age
meadows and high grasslands—old 'marsh'-harrier
cadence within all our histories engage
in the constant, signed by this gene-carrier.

Central Asia 1986

§

If not immeasurable, abstraction Grand Canyon, say
(the Snake's gorge better then), these are the depths where terror lay.
Fool-footing, feeling the updraught, fearing falling all day
amplitude sits heavier than breath-slowing altitude.
Below, immense gulfs swallow proportion to vertigo,
slants soaring hawks show, where markhor dots slowly go
on edges of ledges unseen; on a sheer-screen glued.
And I am, as long ago fossiling child,—petrified
on High Cup Nick's apparently recently-solidified
'intrusive dolerite' crags screaming evil-personified
all that night dreaming restless—that peregrine, this shaheen.
(Still rises to try me, as a trout will to a fly's sheen,
puts aside heights, depths; what dimensions might 'mean'.
Perspectives reach out, but not for any such certitude…)

1986, 2002

Apart Is the Moon There, Is
Obeisance

Flat face of the tiger uptilt, brooding Oriental
felt full in the face Colonel Hay, moon disoriented
reek sweet tomcat bruised foggrassed looming
familiar to this weakness, strength given skin blush blooming
—not the cold nape-fur arisen on end, if that's fear,
hypnotic eye gold-contact drifts down as I draw near
inching, itching to twitch, to touch coup. He is the seer.

(these canyons not coffining 'cultural' advancing
 in Californian indulgence of accultural 'privacy'
 —not confining but confiding and still hiding
 away from what a waying the West is riding…)

Central Asia 1987
revised 2008

§

…There is a rind upon the arid mountains, here and there like the kind
of iron pan, stained, under the peats it's leached from, matter
of which pieces can seem artefacts of ceramic from a potter's mind—
trial pieces or fragments of a tray or mould, or pattern
familiar to my boy-hood imagination on the moors. I'd find
erode in frost and rain. Here such ochreous dust spreads to flatten
the surface as friable as dried peat in a storm of wind
and then as ready to lift even for a short distance
makes a local sandstorm warm so that the worn land surface is skinned
and we are blinded, irritated, wait. Nerves shorn, some younger men
are anxious to go round; a veteran won't get lost, and laughs at them!…

(As) Going to meet E.P.
about 14 years earlier

wind and its sand cloud swallowed into land aloud
of the length of its own chasm, canyon, scar across
strata themselves the wind laid down chronology
faithful as laggar, groundswell hugging albatross
polishing sandblast—but ineffective the stanzas
the saker shows up, he who flies the length out of sight,
as indifferent and lesser, of a minor geomorphology.

pitting and grooving elongate windscars that first Hedin
brought to geologists' attention from here in Turkestan
little scarps needed, even, as must be by the caravan
whose aeons of travel have been thus consonant vowel-leading
scaled-up erosion by prevailing wind-direction:
fringed scarf blowing going to see Mr Pound
how does such clown dare cut a gash in *his* time
attrition is mutual wear of the particles, not the form seen as the map
       is (spinned) finished
Yardang is spun yarn long as the wind
but the academics insist wind can't lift sand even a metre
haven't been here with a wind of sand in the teeth; ablation
blasting the pillars and faces this saker graces, defaces
(temporary stains, where his cousin the gyr paints saltpetre
his pediments white forever despite ice and wet weather!)

Yet the saker and the maker, laggar and makar
whatever their weight might make out of weaker materials
silly lacustrine silts can be undercut to tumble well enough
little concretions defoliated layer by layer of such poor stuff
any ventifract from the real poet's table must be facetted
by the same forces as his magnum opus; as this yardang
went for centuries un-mapped, though Polo may have known it!

Central Asia, 1986

www.ingramcontent.com/pod-product-compliance
Lightning Source LLC
Chambersburg PA
CBHW031155160426
43193CB00008B/381